Understanding Faith

So You Can

Move Your Mountain

Unless otherwise noted, all scripture taken from the King James Version of the Bible. Scriptures marked KJV are taken from the KING JAMES VERSION (KJV): KING JAMES VERSION, public domain.

Scriptures marked MKJV are taken from the MODERN KING JAMES VERSION (MKJV): Scripture taken from the Holy Bible, MODERN KING JAMES VERSION copyright© 1962—1998 by Jay P. Green, Sr. Used by permission of the copyright holder.

Scriptures marked CEV are taken from the CONTEMPORARY ENGLISH VERSION (CEV): Scripture taken from the CONTEMPORARY ENGLISH VERSION copyright© 1995 by the American Bible Society. Used by permission.

Scriptures marked ERV Taken from the HOLY BIBLE: EASY-TO-READ VERSION © 2001 by Bible League International. and used by permission.

Scripture taken from the Literal Translation of the Holy Bible (LITV) Copyright © 1976 - 2000 By Jay P. Green, Sr.
Used by permission of the copyright holder.

Scriptures marked BBE are taken from the 1965 Bible in Basic English. Public Domain.

Understanding Faith So You Can Move Your Mountain
ISBN: 978-1-73276884-0
Editor: Dee Farrell

Copyright ©Flying Eagle Publications 2020.
Flyingeaglepublications.com
Cover images by Kyle Johnson courtesy of Unsplash.
Cover design by Flying Eagle Publications.

All Rights Reserved under International Copyright Law. No part of this book may be reproduced or transmitted in any form or by any means.

Understanding Faith

So You Can

Move Your Mountain

Flying Eagle Publications

First...

Welcome to our Foundations of the Faith series of books. You can find more of our titles at https://www.flyingeaglepublications.com. Please consider leaving a review wherever you discovered the book or send us an email to let us know if you enjoyed it. You can also join our community by signing up for the blog or liking us on Facebook.

In this particular teaching, you will learn about faith, what it is and why we need to live by it to please God. But first, a story...or two.

Nurse and nutritionist Vonya Currey[1] was diagnosed with cancer and chose the Gerson Therapy as her treatment. With its whole body approach to encourage natural healing, the therapy involved a rigorous routine of supplements, enemas and a strict diet of organic grains, vegetables and juices. Vonya became a slave to the process. But it wasn't working for her. Her condition worsened.

Then she discovered the website of a preacher who taught healing. When she finally understood how faith for healing worked, the cancer left her body. It took months of struggle to grasp the truth, but she did, and when she did, it was as easy as knowing God personally and allowing His word to convince her heart that what He said He would do, He would do for her.

---

[1] "Nurse Healed of Cancer," You Tube video, 15:13, posted by Andrew Wommack, May 12,2020, https://www.youtube.com/watch?v=UORspHBuWus&list=PLOER0yhdOW6DZpBV0c_IHqLK6O-io2OVO.

In 2017, almost 600,000 people died of cancer in the United States. Vonya Currey wasn't one of them.

Todd White[2] was delivered from drug addiction and emotional problems when he understood who Jesus really is and who he is in Jesus. Today he shares that story, and miracles happen. The blind see. The lame walk.

Other people tell their stories of healing, deliverance and financial provision. They are people from all types of backgrounds and their testimonies vary, but they all have one thing in common: they had to understand what Jesus willingly did for them.

What you are about to learn many believers have labeled the word of faith movement or think it is New Age meets Christianity. Some even call it the American gospel. It is none of those things. It is the Bible in its own words, with its original meanings sans religious tradition.

You are about to learn what Jesus taught His disciples and what the early church knew. These truths have never been lost. They've been kept alive by a faithful chain of believers, by a God who's nudged

---

[2] "Todd White- My Testimony," You Tube video, 1:30:35, posted by Todd White-Lifestyle Christianity, June 7, 2015, https://www.youtube.com/watch?v=CsnMTWxFNRU.

us to remember them, by the burning fire of the Spirit who watches over us.

Ready? Let's begin.

For we walk by faith, not by sight.

2 Corinthians 5:7

Chapter 1

What Faith Is

The world's definition of faith is taking a blind leap and wishing what you hope for happens, that what you hope is true is true. That is not what the Bible says faith is.

You might have heard that faith is important in the Bible. It is. So important God tells us we cannot please Him without it.

It is critical then we understand what it is.

There are six Hebrew words that help define the concept of the biblical idea of faith. One Hebrew word used for faith is *'âman*. The first time it is used is in Genesis 15:6 concerning Abraham. "And he believed [*'âman*] in the LORD; and he counted it to him for righteousness."

There are several meanings and forms for *'âman* that build upon each other. According to *Gesenius' Hebrew-Chaldee Lexicon*, it means to sustain or support as in carrying a child and one who guards and nourishes. This can be seen in Psalm 31:23. "... The LORD protects the faithful..."

The *Lexicon* continues with these definitions:
- to be or make firm and unshaken like one you can lean on;
- to be established; faithful, trustworthy, sure;
- to be certain, sure of the word of God;
- to be found true;
- to be founded, firm and stable like a firm place where you can drive in a nail;
- to be of long continuance, steadfast; to trust to believe;
- to stand firm.

Strong's Exhaustive Concordance adds pillars and supporters of the door. This is interesting in light of Revelation 3:12 where the faithful make up the pillars supporting the temple. The image is stability, firmness, dependability and certainty.

We can see the definitions of 'âman demonstrated by what Abraham does next in the verses that follow Genesis 15:6. We know Abraham was sure of God's word to him and depended on it because he did what God told him to do. That is, he sacrificed the required animals and arranged them as God had instructed. "Abram brought the animals to God, cut them in half, and placed the halves opposite each other in two rows; but he did not cut up the birds." (Genesis 15:10)

This was done in preparation of making a covenant or a contract with God. If Abraham would not have believed God to be trustworthy, he would not have entered into an agreement with Him. (You can

What Faith Is

read more about Abraham and God's covenant with him in *From Abram to Abraham* by Flying Eagle Publications.)

God reminded a new generation of Israelites of His faithfulness to them with an image of a father carrying his child. If you remember, this is the definition of *'âman* according to the *Gesenius' Hebrew-Chaldee Lexicon*. God said, "And in the wilderness, where thou hast seen how that the LORD thy God bare thee, as a man doth bear his son, in all the way that ye went, until ye came into this place." Yet in spite of God's actions, Israel refused to believe (*'âman*) Him. (Deuteronomy 1:31-32)

Another Hebrew word used for faith is *'ĕmûnâh*. It can be used to mean firmness, security and faithfulness in fulfilling a promise. Here are a few examples:

> But Moses' hands were heavy. Then they took a stone and put it under him, and he sat on it; and Aaron and Hur supported his hands, one on one side and one on the other. Thus his hands were steady [*'ĕmûnâh*] until the sun set. (Exodus 17:12)

> "The Rock! His work is perfect, For all His ways are just; A God of faithfulness [*'ĕmûnâh*] and without injustice, Righteous and upright is He. (Deuteronomy 32:4)

> Moreover, they did not require an accounting from the men into whose hand they gave the money to pay to those who did the work, for they dealt faithfully [*'ĕmûnâh*]. (2Kings 12:15)

> Mattithiah, one of the Levites, who was the firstborn of Shallum the Korahite, had the responsibility [*'ĕmûnâh*] over the things which were baked in pans. (1Chronicles 9:31)

These definitions and verses reveal faith involves two parties working in union with each other. Both sides have contracted responsibilities of steadfastness, loyalty and trust.

For example, Moses told the general of the Israelite army that he would hold up the staff of God while the army was in battle. Moses' expectation was God would help them when He saw the staff raised. God did as Moses asked, and each supported the other, Moses by keeping the staff raised and God by providing victory.

Likewise, those receiving money in 2 Kings 12:15 were given their task and trusted with it because they had a reputation of being faithful. Both parties acted to support each other's trust. This support is seen over and over in the Bible and called trust.

It is important to understand faith happens between two parties and each has a role to play. Abraham did not ignore his part. God did not ignore His. Moses did not sit on a rock hoping God would help. Abraham and Moses supported God by their actions.

In other words, they cooperated with God by acting on His promise to help and trusted Him to follow through on His word. That is the image of biblical faith. It is why the Bible says God watches over His word to perform it (Jeremiah 1:12), and that His word is sure. "Heaven and earth shall pass away: but my words shall not pass away." (Luke 21:33)

The Old Testament shows us faith is not primarily a mental activity. It involves action that follows a decision to trust. "The innocent, the holy have a firm attachment to God and an undisturbed confidence in the divine promises of God."[1] Then we read about this confidence by what the person does next.

Take for example the Levites on the shore of the River Jordan near Jericho. According to Todd Bolen's article, "Seven Fascinating Facts about Crossing the Jordan River[2]," while the northern stretch of the river was easier to cross, the southern part was deep and turbulent. God instructed Joshua (Joshua 3) to have the Levites carrying the ark to step into the water first and the waters would stop so the Israelites could cross the river.

Sounds easy right? But the river had overflowed its banks and the swift current swirled and tumbled

---

[1] Keil & Delitzsch Commentary on the Old Testament, Habakkuk 2:4.

[2] Todd Bolen, "Seven Fascinating Facts about Crossing the Jordan River," BiblePlaces, August 17, 2016. https://www.bibleplaces.com/blog/2016/08/seven-fascinating-facts-about-crossing/

before them. They had to choose between trusting God's word that the waters would part and then act by stepping into the water, or turn back like their parents had done at the border of the Promised Land. (Numbers 13-14) They chose to trust and acted on it. God responded by piling up the water like at the crossing of the Red Sea in Exodus 14.

This is the principle stated in Habakkuk 2:4. "...but the just shall live (*châyâh*) by his faith ['*ĕmûnâh*]." There will be action. The writer of Hebrews refers to this verse when he says, "The just shall live by faith." (10:38)

The just, *tsaddîyq*, are the righteous. They will be made whole, repaired, restored and made alive (*châyâh*) by their faith. This is an echo of Abraham's verse where God counted him righteous because he believed.

Let's briefly look at the other Hebrew words used for faith.

Bâṭach is a word used for trust. It is a confident assurance so that you feel secure, safe and without a care. This is the idea Peter wanted to communicate when he said cast your cares on God. (1Peter 5:7)

Mibṭâch is related to *bâṭach* and means confidence, trust and security. *Châsâh* is a word for trust as in fleeing to a place of refuge. Psalm 91:4 says, "He shall cover thee with his feathers, and under his wings shalt thou trust [*châsâh*]." *Machăseh* derives from *châsâh* and is a shelter or refuge. "God is our refuge [*machăseh*] and strength, a very present help in trouble." (Psalm 46:1)

Gâlal means to roll. We roll our cares or commit something to God because we trust Him as in Psalm

37:5. "Commit [*gâlal*] thy way unto the LORD; trust also in him; and he shall bring it to pass." *Yâchal* is to wait in trust with a confident expectation of good. "For I hope [*yâchal*] in You, O LORD; You will answer, O Lord my God." (Psalm 38:15)[3]

Each of these definitions implies God's good character. He will act on your behalf to save, rescue, protect, help and deliver. The definitions also assume humility on your part— you don't know how to rescue yourself. But your confidence in God brings you a reward when you run to Him in an attitude of humble trust.

To make firm or to establish is part of the definition of faith. The Bible shows us this when it says Abraham was fully persuaded. (Romans 4:21) When you are persuaded, you are sure. You can believe. You are then confident and able to trust.

Becoming persuaded takes time and must come first. Actually before you pray. It is pondering God's word and considering it. It is allowing the word to speak to you. When this happens, something changes deep within you in your spirit. This is why faith is called a spiritual force because being in faith is a condition of your spirit. It is not of the mind or a theological position.

Faith is not a movement or a denomination. It is the anchor of being fully persuaded, confident that what you believe is going to happen despite your im-

---

[3] *Rechats* is another word for trust. It is a Babylonian word that means rely, and it is only used once for trust in Daniel 3:28. Nebuchadnezzar used it to praise God after God rescued Shadrach, Meshach and Abednego from the fiery furnace.

mediate circumstances. It is the image of Jonah, who in the belly of the whale, could look at his surroundings and call them lying vanities.

But do you see that persuasion in the wrong thing is also faith? If you trust in words of defeat, are confident that your circumstances could never change, then you have set your trust, your faith, in failure. Fear energizes this type of faith. In fact, fear is faith. Job witnessed this when he said what he feared came upon him.

This brings us to an important point. Faith is a force that can work for you or against you. Faith just is. Like a law of the universe. If you understand how it works, how to use it, you can see miracles.

Hebrews 11:1 is the New Testament verse most Christians quote when asked what faith is. It says, "Now faith is the substance of things hoped for, the evidence of things not seen." But few actually understand the full meaning of this passage.

Faith in the New Testament's Greek is *pistis*, persuasion, conviction, reliance, constancy, assurance, belief, fidelity. Most English speakers think of faith as a noun, but its Greek primitive root is a verb that means to make fast or bind.

In their entry for the English word faith, *Holman's Bible Dictionary* states that it derives from a French word meaning loyalty, but it became belief in Middle English and progressed to mean an intellectual agreement with a statement. Eventually the verb form of faith disappeared from English.

But in the Old Testament and the New Testament, faith includes the idea of support by action. Biblically it requires action. It is not a mental activity alone. James 2:26 says, "For as the body without the spirit is dead, so faith [*pistis*, conviction]without works [*ergon*, an act] is dead also."

Biblical faith is NOT passive.

The verse in Hebrews tells us faith is the substance, *hypostasis*, the foundation, the setting under support, the assurance, that which has actual existence, the confidence and firm trust.

Faith is the evidence, *elegchos*, the proof by which a thing is tested. According to *Strong's*, *elegchos* means "that by which invisible things are proved (and we are convinced of their reality)."

Notice that your faith is your proof whatever you are believing for is yours. Allow this to encourage you when your circumstances are telling you the opposite.

One more word needed to be defined in this verse is hope. Hope is *elpizō*, expectation. The English meaning of the word hope used to be the same as the biblical definition, according to Noah Webster's 1828 *American Dictionary Of The English Language*. In fact, it informed the reader that hope has a different meaning than desire or wish.

Modern dictionaries, however, define hope as a want or a desire, and they list "confident trust" as an archaic definition. In other words, hope doesn't mean what it used to.

When you read the word hope in the Bible, say "confident expectation" out loud because that is hope's biblical definition.

Let's write Hebrews 11:1 with its original meanings: Now your heart persuaded conviction and reliance on God's word and loyalty to His faithfulness is the setting under support of total confidence and the proof of the invisible things you can't see yet but confidently expect.

Biblical faith is not a passive belief that God exists. Real positive faith is convinced God is real, His words are true and that He is faithful and willing to help you or reward you when you come to Him. In fact, you expect Him to deliver.

This is the faith that pleases God. "But without faith it is impossible to please him: for he that cometh to God must believe that he is, and that he is a rewarder of them that diligently seek [*ekzēteō*, search out, investigate, crave, worship] him." (Hebrews 11:6)

This is the Bible definition of faith and what we are to be exercising now before eternity as the context of Habakkuk 2:4 shows. The just live by their faith.

Notice that belief in Jesus is not mentioned in Hebrews 11:1. But the New Testament is clear that it is because of Jesus' death and resurrection that we in our day can know all of God's promises are yes and so be it (amen) to those who trust Him. (2Corinthians 1:20)

God has already said yes to every promise and blessing you see in His word. What you need to know is how to receive what He has freely given.

Going Deeper

Define faith.

Explain the phrase faith expects.

What is the biblical definition of hope?

What is the most important thing you've learned from this chapter?

How will you apply that new knowledge to your life?

Begin to praise God for teaching you about faith. Ask God to reveal to you places in your life where you need to be persuaded concerning His truth. Write down what He shows you.

Chapter 2

Why God Uses Faith

The simplest reason as to why God uses faith is because it is how He Himself works. It is how He created the earth and everything on it in accordance with Genesis 1.

Faith works miracles on earth now, but it is not miraculous in the spiritual world. Faith's laws are how that world runs. To us it seems amazing, and it is because it is beyond our natural surroundings. But in the spiritual world, it is the way things *are*.

You might wonder then how could something God created work against us? What many don't understand is they have an enemy called *satan*. You can learn much more about him and how he became your enemy in *Born Again: Not Just For Heaven*.

Satan has no power to invent his own laws. He has to use the ones God already created. So, he uses the force of faith because he wants you to have faith in his works which are disease, calamity, chaos, defeat, etc. These are things associated with his kingdom of darkness as Jesus called it.

Faith as God intended it, focused on His desire to bless you, is absolute confidence that His word is true and He will perform what He said He would do because He is good and will act for your best interest. It is to become fully persuaded in these things.

We then prove our trust by what we say and do. When we exhibit this kind of faith, we please God because it is the basis of acting and doing whatever we are to receive from Him, whether it is salvation, provision, wisdom or healing, ministering to someone else, etc.

In the New Testament, Jesus revealed God's principles to His followers. For example, He said when we give, it is given to us. He also said with the measure we use, it is measured to us. God's principles are part of a government called the kingdom or the kingdom of heaven. Faith is one of the foundational principles of God's kingdom.

But there is another kingdom at work on the earth, and it is called the kingdom of darkness. (There is no third kingdom where man makes up the rules.) Man lives and moves and has his being out of one of the two kingdoms.[1]

Man is naturally born into the kingdom of darkness and only becomes a citizen of the kingdom of heaven through complete trust in Jesus and confessing Him as Savior and Lord according to Romans 10:10. Receiving salvation is the result of being fully persuaded in Je-

---

[1] For more about this read *Born Again:Not Just For Heaven* by Flying Eagle Publications.

sus' death and resurrection for the purpose of our forgiveness whereby we then become the righteousness of God after we confess this conviction. We make our choice by believing and saying.

This pattern of being made righteous is still the same as Noah or Abraham had to exhibit in the Old Testament. They had to believe, say and then act on that belief. This is what faith looks like.

For example, Noah had to trust God, speak and then act by building the ark on dry ground before rain existed. Abraham had to trust God; then he had to speak and act so he could make a legal agreement with God to bless him and give him a son.

On the other hand, unbelief results in unrighteousness. If you doubt the existence of God or His good character or the absolute truth and accuracy of God's word, then you are placing your trust in some other source connected to the kingdom of darkness and its claims. This is faith in Satan and what he has to offer.

Doubt is not being persuaded. You are unconvinced because you are considering something else more valuable. When it applies to God, it prevents you from receiving from Him all that He has for you.

Not because He doesn't want to give to you, but because you are outside His standard of faith. God does not violate His own words or established laws. He doesn't change. He is not a liar, nor is there any shadow of turning in Him. (James 1:17)

Therefore doubt is a roadblock to your victory. When you speak it and act on it by your behavior, you will not receive God's blessings, but Satan's curses of defeat and failure. Let's take a closer look at doubt for a minute, since doubt can be complete or partial.

For example, you may believe in God but not the accuracy of His word. Therefore your trust is in the teachings of evolution or some other theory for your standard of history. You may believe there is a God but He doesn't heal. Therefore, your absolute trust is in the medical field. You may not believe God is willing to help you with your finances, so you only rely on your job and the world's financial system.

The point is you doubt God because you believe in something else. You wrestle with other thoughts which come with emotions and feelings that convince you God's word cannot be trusted in your circumstance. Those other thoughts and feelings usually stir up fear as you fixate on your problem. This is how you know you are not in the God kind of faith.

But Abraham came to a point of complete persuasion in God's promise to give him a son despite his dire circumstances: his wife had never conceived and she was almost ninety and he was almost a hundred. The Bible says Abraham considered not his own body.

> And being not weak in faith, he considered [*katanoeō*, to observe fully] not his own body now dead, when he was about an hundred years old, neither yet the deadness of Sara's womb: He staggered not at the promise of God through

unbelief; but was strong in faith, giving glory to God; And being fully persuaded that, what he had promised, he was able also to perform."

(Romans 4:19-21)

He believed God as his only source for truth, deliverance, protection, provision, and he trusted God to be honest and faithful to do what He promised. Abraham miraculously received his desires. The lesson learned is you cannot doubt if you don't consider other things. We are to fix our eyes on God with a steady constant gaze. (Hebrews 12:2)

God counted Abraham's trust in Him as righteousness. Today we become righteous by coming to the same fully persuaded conviction about Jesus and His work for us on the cross to forgive our sins. And, because of Jesus we can receive the miracles we desire. We just need to understand how God works with our trust in Him.

When Jesus was asked what people needed to do to work the works of God, Jesus told them to believe. "Jesus answered and said unto them, 'This is the work of God, that ye believe on him whom he hath sent.' " (John 6:29) When you believe something, you will act accordingly.

God's kingdom only opens its door to those who make an active decision to join it. If you don't join God's kingdom through faith in Jesus and operating in His ways, you remain in the kingdom of darkness by default and subject to Satan's curses. God will not force you to do anything. He has given you a free will, and He will not take back what He has given. He respects your freedom.

Faith exists for your benefit and allows you to make your own decision. It is what opens the door to God. When you decide to believe God and accept Jesus, God makes you righteous. "For he hath made him to be sin for us, who knew no sin; that we might be made the righteousness of God in him." (2Corinthians 5:2)

Faith is your act of making your decision known, the decision you made out of your freewill and whatever you allowed to persuade you and make you confident. Faith is your choice acted out. For good, or for bad.

If you have accepted Jesus into your heart as your Savior and Lord, nothing is impossible for you because everything God promised is yours for the taking. Jesus said faith takes. Let's find out how to do that.

Going Deeper

Why does God use faith?

Why does God require believers to live by faith?

What are the two kingdoms operating on the earth? Describe them.

Explain doubt.

What is a consequence of doubt?

How are faith and freewill connected?

Praise God that His ways are good. Give Him thanks because He desires to speak to you and hear all of your concerns. Take time to allow the Holy Spirit to cleanse your heart. Repent of any sin or unforgiveness. Pray in tongues. Share what is on your mind with God. Ask Him what He thinks of these things and write down what He says. Ask Him what His concerns are and make them a prayer.

Chapter 3

How Faith Operates

Here is the part about faith most Christians don't understand. If they did, there would be a lot less suffering, unsatisfied believers.

Galatians 5:6 tells us **faith works by love**. It is effective when we understand God's love toward us. This verse is talking about Jesus' love and not what we do to make ourselves worthy. Love compelled God to extend mercy in the form of His grace for salvation. (Ephesians 2:8) It is why love is considered the greatest among faith, confident expectation [hope] and love. (1Corinthians 13:13)

The word translated works in Galatians 5:6 is *energeō*, active, efficient, effectual. Love is *agapē*, the highest level of love that exists. This is God's love and He gives it to men. For a picture of *agapē* read 1Corinthians 13:4-8. You may recognize this as the love chapter, and it is taught to us to show how we should love others as Jesus commanded in Mark 12:31.

But we also need to *agapē* God as Jesus commanded in Mark 12:30. About the two commands Jesus said, "There is none other commandment greater than these." Take time to reflect on the verses below and ask yourself, "Is this how I love God?"

> Love is kind and patient, never jealous, boastful, proud, or rude. Love isn't selfish or quick tempered. It doesn't keep a record of wrongs that others do. Love rejoices in the truth, but not in evil. Love is always supportive, loyal, hopeful, and trusting. Love never fails!
> (1Corinthians 13:5-8 CEV)

Read the verses again and ask yourself, "Is this how I believe God loves me?"

Jesus is the image of *agapē*. He is compelled by love to show mercy. His healing miracles show and tell this repeatedly. He was moved by compassion, a tender pity or sympathy, so He healed them all the Bible tells us. He would do the same today. His love compelled Him to die on a cross for all men, knowing many would reject His love towards them.

Until you understand God's great love extended toward you, you will never be ready to trust Him. Your faith becomes effective and active when you receive the *agapē* love of God. He searches for someone He can bless with this love. "For the eyes of the LORD run to and fro throughout the whole earth, to shew himself strong in the behalf of them whose heart is perfect toward him." (2Chronicles 16:9)

Strong is *châzaq* and it means to fasten upon in order to cure, help, encourage, repair and strengthen. Perfect is *shâlêm*, to be complete, whole or perfect. Another meaning is friendly or peaceable which is interesting because *shâlêm* is from the verb *shalam* which means to be at peace with or in covenant with.

Jesus said He only did what the Father [God] showed Him to do. Jesus looked for whom He could help. He said of the centurion's faith that He hadn't seen any like it in Israel. He was looking because He had a desire to bless people. He does the same today.

The *Orthodox Jewish Bible* interprets *shâlêm* as wholehearted. In the New Testament, perfect is defined as without fear. "There is no fear in love[*agapē*]; but perfect love [*agapē*] casteth out fear: because fear hath torment. He that feareth is not made perfect in love." (1John 4:18) Perfect is the Greek *teleios*, complete.

Fear is faith in Satan's works. Like faith it too is a spiritual force, and God did not give it to Christians. "For God hath not given us the spirit of fear; but of power, and of love, and of a sound mind." (2Timothy 1:7) God doesn't give it because it torments you and breeds unbelief.

God has already extended His *agapē* love toward you. He is waiting for you to receive it, and when you do, you will be able to resist the fear of failure and the doubts inspired by fear about His willingness to help you. That God is able to help you is common knowledge. You believe in His power. But do you believe in His love for you?

Faith doesn't work by His power. It goes into effect when you get a glimpse of His love. Becoming perfect [complete] in *agapē* love is what gives you boldness [*parrhēsia*]. (1John 4:17)

The next misunderstanding concerning faith is not knowing you play a role in receiving what you've asked for. Many think it is all up to God. But He requires your cooperation with Him. Your part is to know His will and believe that you have received what you have asked for. His part is to act on your complete trust in obedience to your belief in Him and His word to you.

Jesus stated the principle of how faith works to His disciples, and it has been recorded so all generations could learn it. One morning, Jesus and His disciples were walking to Jerusalem and Jesus was hungry. He saw a fig tree with leaves which indicated it should have some fruit on it.

But it didn't. There was something wrong with the tree. The verse says He answered it which means He addressed its perverse condition (compared to the way it was created to function). "And Jesus answered and said unto it, 'No man eat fruit of thee hereafter for ever.' And his disciples heard it." (Mark 11:14)

Later that day, they passed by the tree as they returned to the place where they were staying. But in the morning as they made their way back into Jerusalem, they saw the fig tree withered from the roots, which means there was no other reason for it to have dried up. The disciples were amazed it had happened and so quickly.

How Faith Operates

Then Jesus told them something more amazing. He said they could do the same thing. "And answering, Jesus said to them, 'Have faith of God. For truly I say to you, Whoever says to this mountain, Be taken up and be thrown into the sea, and does not doubt in his heart, but believes that what he says will happen, it will be to him, whatever he says.' " (Mark 11:22-23 LITV)

Many translations say Jesus told them to have faith in God, but the correct translation is have the faith of God. This is important because Jesus was teaching them this is how God-faith works. According to *Adam Clarke's Commentary on the Bible*, this can be understood as saying, have strong faith, or this is the strongest faith. Jesus was saying, "Here is how you can do what I do."

This is the principle: believe in your heart you have received then speak what you want to happen.

The principle is referred to many times in the Bible. For example, 2Corithians 4:13 connects believing and speaking with the spirit of faith. "But having the same spirit of faith, according to what has been written, 'I believed, therefore I spoke,' we also believe, therefore we also speak." This is the same process by which we receive salvation. "For with the heart man believeth unto righteousness; and with the mouth confession is made unto salvation." (Romans 10:10)

Notice that believing what has been done and then confessing brings about your salvation. You are not saved then you confess it. The confessing is half of the action required for you to become saved; thus, "confession is made unto salvation." The 1965 *Bible in Basic English* (BBE) translation says, "For with the heart man has faith to get righteousness, and with the mouth he says that Jesus is Lord to get salvation."

This is the pattern of how your faith works. You believe to the point of being fully persuaded so there is no doubt, and then you speak. For example, you become fully persuaded and believe in your heart God wants to heal your sore knee after reading Scriptures about healing. You are convinced He has provided you with healing. You receive it. Then you speak to your knee, "Be healed."

After laying out the principle of faith, Jesus applied it to praying. "Therefore I say unto you, What things soever ye desire, when ye pray, believe that ye receive them, and ye shall have them." (Mark 11:24) Let's read the same verse in simplified English. "So I tell you to ask for what you want in prayer. And if you believe that you have received those things, then they will be yours." (ERV)

Here is an important part of the principle. Did you notice that you need to believe you have received when you pray? *Lambanō* is the Greek word translated receive, and it means to take. This is why some Bibles use the word receive in the past tense to convey the idea that God has given you what you want; He is not resisting you.

According to *Strong's Greek Dictionary*, other definitions for *lambanō* are to take in order to carry away, to get hold of, to claim, of that which when taken is not let go, to receive what is offered. *Vine's Expository Dictionary of New Testament Words* defines *lambanō* as accept, take, hold, receive, "to receive as merely a self-prompted action."

You are so assured you have what you asked for that you consider it done. "And this is the confidence that we have in him, that, if we ask any thing according to his will, he heareth us: And if we know that he hear us, whatsoever we ask, we know that we have the petitions that we desired of him." (1John 5:14-15) Confidence (*parrhēsia*) is all out spokenness, boldness.

God's will is salvation. The Old Testament Hebrew word for salvation is *yesha`*. It is found in places like 2Samuel 22, Psalm 18 and 27. It means safety, welfare, deliverance, liberty, prosperity, rescue and victory. It included the idea of healing. Salvation in the Old Testament focused mainly on physical deliverance, but spiritual rescue was promised. *Yesha`* is the Hebrew form of Jesus. The Old Testament concept of salvation is brought into the New Testament when Jesus revealed His purpose in Luke 4:18-19.

New Testament words for salvation are *soteria* and *sozo*. According to *Strong's*, *sozo* means "to save, keep safe and sound, to rescue from danger or destruction one (from injury or peril), to save a suffering one (from perishing), i.e. one suffering from disease, to make well, heal, restore to health, to preserve one who is in danger of destruction, to save or rescue, to save in the technical biblical sense." *Soteria* means rescue, safety, deliver, health and salvation.

Religion will tell you those things are waiting for you when you get to heaven, but here on the earth we must endure. Jesus didn't say that to the people coming to Him for help. He healed them all. He supplied fishermen with fish and then money to pay their taxes. You won't need this kind of help when you get to heaven.

Jesus died so you could have healing. This isn't just in a spiritual sense; it includes physical healing. It is why He told the people, "Which is easier to say? Your sins are forgiven or rise up and walk?" (Luke 5:23) Jesus fulfilled all God's requirements, removing all sin from us thereby making us able to inherit all God's blessings. God has prepared a table for us *in the presence of our enemies*. Will we have enemies in heaven? No!

Salvation is yours now and in heaven. When Jesus taught His disciples to pray, He told them to pray God's will on earth as in heaven. (Matthew 6:10) Heaven on earth. Why? Because that is God's will for you as far as we may obtain it on earth, but it isn't guaranteed if you don't know how faith works.

Most of what we ask for, God has already given us through salvation. This is why we can be confident we may take what He has provided. God tells us we may ask for wisdom. He tells us He wants to supply all our needs. So unless you are asking to rob a bank, murder someone, be a successful liar or cheat, or some other crazy immoral request, you can be sure God will listen to you.

One of the first things to note is faith doesn't beg. It is sure of the outcome. It is confident in the Giver.

Begging implies you have to convince the one you are begging to give you what you desire because they do not want to give it to you.

A begging prayer is an uncertain prayer. But you need to convince your own heart, not God. You need to know what He has already provided for you in *agapē* love and what He desires to give you. Knowing these things will put you on firm ground and give you the ability to believe.

Many Christians ask God to give them more faith. But faith only comes by hearing God's word. "So then faith cometh by hearing, and hearing by the word of God." (Romans 10:17) When you read the Bible, you hear what He wants to do for you.

The word speaks to you. Jesus said His words are spirit and life. (John 6:63) God's word, His *rhēma*, is alive. Luke 1:37 says, "With God nothing [literally, no *rhēma*] is impossible. No word is impossible.

It is hard to trust someone if you do not know if they are willing to help you. But the Bible tells the story of a leper who bowed down in front of Jesus one day and said, "Lord if you are willing, You are able to make me clean."

This is the classic prayer of most Christians. They know God is able, but will He? For them? Jesus answered the question for everyone for all time because He is the same yesterday today and forever. (Hebrews 13:8)

Leprosy was one of the worst diseases of Jesus' time with no cure and no hope. Lepers had to separate from society and were not allowed to touch others.

People were not allowed to touch lepers either. They all had to abide by extreme social distancing laws. But Jesus answered the leper with *agapē* and touched Him. "And stretching out the hand, He touched him, saying, I will! Be cleansed! And instantly the leprosy departed from him." (Luke 5: 12-13 LITV) The leper heard Jesus' words of compassion, and he was healed.

Another time, Jesus was in a synagogue when He saw a woman with a deformed back. He saw her and called her to come to Him. He was looking and wanted to free her. Just think if she would not have cooperated. But she did and was healed that day after eighteen years of being crippled. (Luke 13:11-16)

Make it your mission to hear God's words to you that are written in the Bible. Many of those Jesus healed heard about the miracles He had already done. These testimonies gave confidence to those who lowered their paralyzed friend through an opening in a roof, to the woman who braved the crowd to touch the hem of His garment and to a man with an epileptic son.

The Bible is God's announcement of what He has promised to do for you. The first thing to do is seek God for what He has to say about your need or desire. Once you have knowledge of God's will for your situation, you are in a position to convince your heart of this truth.

Take action: Find at least three Scriptures that pertain to your need. Study these verses and any of God's promises that cover your situation.

Take the time to convince your heart on the truth of the promises and the character of the God who made them. Ask God for wisdom and for the Holy Spirit to teach you. Write down what He speaks (His *rhēma*, word) to you. Study John 15:7-16.[1]

Faith is an action of your deepest self. The process may begin by information coming to you through your mind by reading the Bible, but it becomes a conviction when it takes root in your heart. This is why faith is never a blind leap. There is evidence upon which you have based your decision to act.

Jesus used this faith principle when He spoke to a blind beggar. (Mark 10:46-52) He used it when He prayed for Lazarus. Jesus was thanking God for hearing Him while Lazarus was still dead. He spoke things into existence by calling those things that are not as though they are. (Romans 4:17) He did it to the fig tree we learned about, and He spoke of His finished work on the cross before it was finished. (John 17:4)

This principle of believing and confessing may be seen throughout the Bible. Even Jonah, from inside the belly of the whale, had the boldness to say his circumstances were lying vanities and that he would again see the Temple in Israel. It didn't look good, but he got what he said and believed because he understood the mercy and goodness of God.

---

[1] God's commandments are that you believe and accept Jesus, love others as yourself and love God with all your heart, mind, soul and strength.

For you to get what you desire, you must believe you receive when you ask. When you say amen which means so be it, you got it. True faith is in the present– you have "it" whatever "it" is. You are not waiting to get it. Faith uses the sight of an enlightened heart. (Ephesians 1:18) It sees the final result as in your hand. Now it is up to you not to let go of it.

You must stand in the past tenses of God. Faith isn't faith until you know you have received. This is the substance, the setting under support, and the evidence that what is true in the spirit— your healing, protection, provision— will become true in our physical world. It will appear.

Hebrews 10:23 tells you to hold fast to your confession. For those who insist this verse speaks only of salvation, remember the two words used for salvation are *sozo* and *soteria*. Since both words contain the concept of health, protection, deliverance and provision now and in the future, salvation includes most things Christians are praying about.

The point is, remain in a place of faith because God is faithful and He doesn't change His mind about any of His promises. Don't change your words; speak the same things God has spoken over you.

Your firm, unwavering trust must be in God's word alone. Not circumstances, emotions, feelings or the opinions of others. Circumstances are temporary as Abraham, Jonah and a host of blind, lame and sick people found out. Satan will try to shake your confidence by turning your attention to "the facts".

Ten lepers met Jesus outside a town and asked Him to heal them. He told them to go present themselves to the priests. They had to turn away from Jesus while they were still lepers, the "facts", and start walking to show the priests they were healed. What would have happened if they would have looked down at their bodies and said, "This is stupid. I'm not healed. I can't go to the priest. He will think I'm crazy." Besides, a leper went to see the priest after they were healed.

They didn't understand the *believe you have received* principle, but they took Jesus' at His word and set out. They got their healing on the way; it wasn't immediate. Many answers aren't immediate, but they are in motion toward you because they are making their way from the spirit world to the physical one as you believe and obey.

You can make the time your answers are in motion longer or shorter based on what you do after you've prayed. We will study that in the next chapter.

Going Deeper

How does faith work by love?

Did you discover problem areas in your *agapē* love towards God when you read 1 Corinthians 13:4-8? In believing of His *agapē* toward you? Write them down and pray over them. Ask God to teach you about His love.

What is your responsibility concerning faith?

What is the principle of how faith works?

Explain Mark 11:22-24 in your own words.

What do you need to believe when you pray?

How does faith come?

What are two things you should do before you pray?

Why is it important to know God's will for your circumstances?

Praise God that He has already provided for your every need. Make a list of His promises to you and confess them daily. Turn them into a list of thank yous that you speak to God. Submit yourself to Him and speak in tongues. Ask Him what are the works He would like to work for you and through you. Write down what He says and any verses He brings to your mind.

Chapter 4
How to Walk By Faith

The Bible says that honoring and respecting God is the way to have wisdom and knowledge. Humility is required to come to God. "But without faith it is impossible to please Him, for he who comes to God must believe that He is and that He is a rewarder of those who diligently seek Him." (Hebrews 11:6)

For you to live by faith as the righteous do, you must believe God and believe He rewards those who seek Him diligently.

Real faith is not passive. It takes and keeps. The Bible says the violent take the Kingdom by force. (Matthew 11:12) This means everything contained in the Kingdom including all its benefits. We do not fight God for it. He gave it to us. We fight to believe, and we fight against Satan who attempts to deceive us. This is fighting the good fight of faith. (1Timothy 6:12)

Real faith understands you have a part to play and must cooperate with God. Your reward is the result you are believing for. Our prayer is only gas if we believe it is.

He promises if you seek, you will find. If you ask, He will give. The tense of the verbs in this scripture imply ongoing action. "Ask, and it shall be given you; seek, and ye shall find; knock, and it shall be opened unto you: For every one that asketh receiveth; and he that seeketh findeth; and to him that knocketh it shall be opened." (Matthew 7:7-8)

The implication is, "Come often; the door is always open to you." Study this passage and the lesson Jesus taught in Luke 11:1-13 about prayer.

We need to understand what to do after we have asked for and taken our request. The Holy Spirit tells us to "...hold fast the profession of our faith without wavering (for He is faithful who promised)..." (Hebrews 10:23) *Katechō* is translated hold fast and it means to hold down. You can't let your confession escape because it is the way we express our belief.

Satan wants your eyes on symptoms and circumstances. He wants you thinking on these...a lot. He wants you picturing them and playing out their plots of defeat, lack and failure. This is meditating on your problems, and he is aggressive in his efforts toward this goal. He wants your faith to be in failure.

He pushes you to talk about your situation, to confess your doubts, replay what so and so had to say about it. He wakes you up to remind you. He wants your friends decreeing your failure too. "Oh, I wish things would change, but there is no way it will." He puts more pressure on you to give in, to the pain, the threats, the professional opinions.

But if you do these things, you are undoing any prayer you prayed and letting your confession escape. You are like the farmer who planted his seed and then went out and dug it up. No miracle is growing to appear in your world. You dug it up.

Jesus said, "If ye abide in me, and my words abide in you, ye shall ask what ye will, and it shall be done unto you." (John 15:7) Abide is *menō*, to stay, continue, stand, remain. This idea is referred to throughout the Bible. You must keep God's promise to you alive by meditating on it and confessing it.

Faith stands. It remains. It doesn't totter, stagger or waver between opinions. It believes one thing and speaks one thing: the result you want.

For as long as it takes. Faith works by love but it stands and rests in God's power. "That your faith should not stand in the wisdom of men, but in the power of God." (1Corinthians 2:5)

If you don't remain in trust, you hinder, delay or derail God's ability to answer your prayer. Remember, He works by the principles He has established, and faith is one of those principles.

Nothing is impossible with God, but as Jesus said many times it is according to our faith, what we believe. We don't fight against God to get what we want. We fight unbelief.

There can be no doubt at the deepest level. "But let him ask in faith, nothing wavering. For he that wavereth is like a wave of the sea driven with the wind and tossed. For let not that man think that he shall receive any thing of the Lord. A double minded man is unstable in all his ways." (James 1:6-8)

Wavering is the opposite of remaining. It is *diakrinō* and means to withdraw. When you waver–doubt– you withdraw your trust. It is your responsibility to persuade your heart until it can be known that victory is done, so sure you can see it with your imagination.

If doubt riddled thoughts and the feelings attached to them come to your mind they must be refused. This is why you must take the time to convince your heart and be disciplined to keep your trust on God's word only, enlightened by His love for you.

Thoughts of defeat and failure come from your enemy, Satan. He is attempting to steal from you by having you take his thoughts and not rely on God's word. You take a thought when you speak it. But thinking Satan's thoughts, you will look around at your circumstances and be tempted to give up.

This is Satan testing your faith. Your job is to remain constant. "Knowing this, that the trying of your faith worketh patience. [*hupomonē*, endurance, constancy] But let patience have her perfect work, that ye may be perfect and entire, wanting nothing." (James 1:3-4)

If you let go of your confession, if you let go of your trust that you have received and focus on the circumstances, you will fail. "Cast not away therefore your confidence, which hath great recompence of reward. For ye have need of patience [*hupomonē*], that, after ye have done the will of God, ye might receive the promise." (Hebrews 10:35-36)

Casting away your confidence is the image of throwing it overboard. Doing the "will of God" in this verse is not withdrawing but remaining in an attitude of confident expectation and trust, continuing to confess the result you want. The primary way you release faith (confidence, assurance, trust) is by your words. That is why your words will reveal if you are in faith or out of faith. You need to guard every word coming out of your mouth. Do not cooperate with Satan.

"Now the just shall live by faith: but if any man draw back, my soul shall have no pleasure in him." (Hebrews 10:38) Drawing back is *hupostellō* which also means to shrink, to cower, to withdraw. From what are you drawing back? Your trust that God has given you what you've asked for. Do you see that faith is only real faith when you believe you have received?

God doesn't like it when we shrink back from what He's provided. He wants you to pass Satan's testing by remaining in trust of His goodness and willingness to give you what you want. The minute you withdraw trust in God, you exhibit your trust in Satan and in your circumstances. You have exalted them over God.

Are you believing for a wayward child or unbelieving friend? Then be careful to make your words agree with what you want as a final result. Whining and talking of their failures only confirms the opposite of what you want for them. Your words have creative power. Use them for good, not to establish Satan's plans. Satan has planted weeds, corruption of God's word and His creation, on the earth.

The same goes for your health. Don't confess all your ailments and latest bad reports. Speak what you want to happen– what God's word says is true about your health. This is remaining in faith.

Put your effort into praise and thanksgiving. Even while you are hurting. Pain is a strong distraction. Instead of concentrating on it, turn your promise scriptures into praise and do whatever you can despite the pain or difficulty.

Are you desiring a better job or wanting to pay off debt? Study what God says about finances and come into agreement with Him. Start tithing from what you have and begin confessing God's has blessed your finances. Don't speak or think failure.

Saying thank you is what you say after someone gives you what you've asked for. So if you really believe you have received what you've asked for, your response should be thankfulness, gratefulness and praise. The level of your praise shows the level of your trust. Praise often and much.

Praise helps to continue persuading your heart. It builds assurance that what you desire is yours. Praise God and let the eyes of your heart become the sight by which you see your circumstances. F.F. Bosworth said faith is walking by "sight of a better kind."[1]

Fear is an indicator you are slipping. Peter asked to walk on water and began to do it on the words of Jesus. When he surrendered his sight to the waves and felt the wind, he started to sink because he feared. He began to

---

[1] F.F. Bosworth, *Christ the Healer* (Grand Rapids, MI: Chosen Books, 2008),125.

doubt, allowing Satan to take from him what he already had: the ability to walk on water which was his desire.

Jesus said, "Oh you of puny persuasion [*oligopistos*], why did you doubt?" (Matthew 14:28-31 paraphrased) Thankfully, Jesus who is the Author and Finisher of our faith, didn't leave Peter in his state of puny persuasion, and He won't leave us there either. We have the Holy Spirit's help.

Doubt and fear go together. When you start to experience doubt and fear, if you speak in tongues, begin speaking. Choose to praise God. Speak to the thoughts and feelings and tell them to leave. Continue praising God and speak your final result. James 3 tells us our tongue is like the rudder of a ship so chart your course and set it to victory.

Unbelief is undoing your belief. You may have started in faith, but you are also digging it up. Stop the cycle. You only need a speck of faith to accomplish your goal, a mustard seed sized faith, Jesus said. But it requires zero unbelief. Meditate on the verses that promise your victory. Like Abraham, consider nothing else. No thing Satan dangles in front of you. Nothing.

Doubt is not the only hindrance to faith. Remember faith works– becomes active and efficient– by love, love for God and God's love for us. It is our responsibility to be growing in love toward God and others. Therefore anger, strife, unforgiveness, greed, etc. are stumbling blocks to faith.

Jesus taught that unforgiveness can be a hindrance to answered prayers. "And when ye stand praying, forgive, if ye have ought against any: that your Father also which is in heaven may forgive you your trespasses. But if ye do not forgive, neither will your Father which is in heaven forgive your trespasses." (Mark 11:25-26)

Another hindrance to faith, and we have talked about this earlier, is not understanding you have a responsibility to cooperate with God. Many are taught God is sovereign and He has already decided what is going to happen. If you are struggling with this, ask yourself what has God done in His sovereignty? Has He promised blessings? Healing? What does He say in His word about these things? What has He said about you?

God told Isaiah to tell Hezekiah he was going to die of cancer. According to those who teach this soveriegnty message this was God's will. But God was only informing Hezekiah of the facts. Hezekiah's outcome depended on what he did next. Submit? Or, remember God's promises to heal according to Old Testament covenant and ask God to make good on His promise?

Hezekiah asked by reminding God of all he had done. He had obeyed the covenant and honored God. This is called making a demand on the promise. Unlike men, God doesn't make promises He doesn't want to keep. He wants us to remind Him because it is our act of faith. Isaiah didn't even leave the palace before God told him to go back and tell Hezekiah that He heard His prayer and answered it. Did God change His mind? No, He intervened in what would have happened.

Some believe God uses sickness to teach you about

How To Walk By Faith

Him or about His ways. This makes prayer difficult. What if Hezekiah would have believed this? What if the blind men, the ten lepers, or any of those Jesus healed would have believed this? It makes tragedies God's fault because He willed someone to die by disease or disaster. But death was not God's will for man. It was not part of the original creation, and it is not in heaven. The sovereignty doctrine makes people angry with God. It confuses them and makes them targets for Satan because it perverts God's love toward them.

Those who teach the sovereignty doctrine point to the book of Job. But are you Job? He had no covenant promises, no Savior, he wasn't born again and he had no authority over Satan. Is this you?

God is sovereign, but He has chosen in His sovereignty to provide mercy, healing, protection and provision, to give man a free will so he may become an heir, free him from sin and to give him authority and dominion on the earth for a time. (Mark 12 and 13:34; Luke 10:19) We are living in that time. Jesus restored us to our position, and He tells us to ask for what we want Him to do. Then He requires us to believe we have received from Him what we've asked and to remain in that faith.

To walk in faith is to remain steadfast in confident expectation. You must expect to receive your answer. Anticipate. You are not a passive bystander. Therefore guard against any actions or behavior that is a compromise to failure.

Does this mean not taking medicine? No, but it does mean everytime you take it, you are praising God that His word is a better medicine because it has healed you. You do this until your healing appears.

What if we fail to receive? Does this make faith of no effect? No, it doesn't. It means we failed.

"For what if some did not believe? shall their unbelief make the faith of God without effect? God forbid: yea, let God be true, but every man a liar." (Romans 3:3-4) Did Peter give up? No, he didn't. He failed more than once. Did Thomas, Doubting Thomas, give up? No.

So just keep going. Continue talking to God and listening. Volunteer to learn. Like Peter. Like Thomas.

Take Action: Submit to God and resist Satan. Forgive anyone you need to forgive. Thank God for His word, His goodness and His grace. Ask according to His word and thank Him for giving you your answer.

Keep His word in front of your eyes according to Proverbs 4:20-23. Speak to your circumstances the truth of God's will concerning them. Stay in praise and thanksgiving until your answer shows up in the physical world. This is doing the will of God according to Hebrews 10:36.

God wants you to succeed. He is willing to help you do it. Ask questions if you get stuck. Then do what He tells you to do.

Let's sum up what we've learned.
- Faith comes when you hear God's word and know what His will is.
- Faith is being fully persuaded in your heart so that you are convinced and fully trust God's word and God's good character.
- Faith works through love.
- Faith believes it has received.
- Faith takes; it doesn't beg.
- Faith speaks.
- Faith is not passive; it acts on what it professes to believe and has received.
- Faith remains and speaks only what God says because it has received.
- Faith is thankful.
- Faith praises God for the answer daily.
- Faith considers only God and His word.
- Faith never responds to fear; it resists it.
- Faith stands steadfast in expectation.

Here is one more Scripture to speak over yourself: "But [you] are not of them who draw back unto perdition; but of them that believe to the saving of the soul." (Hebrews 10:39)

We hope as you meditate on the verses given and spend time with God you will gain understanding in all that He wants for you. This is our prayer for you: "Now the God of hope fill you with all joy and peace in believing, that ye may abound in hope, through the power of the Holy Ghost." (Romans 15:13)

Going Deeper

Why is it important to hold fast to your confession?

What does it mean to remain?

What does wavering mean?

Who tests you?

How do you handle doubt?

What are hindrances to faith?

Praise God for His goodness and for the gift of the Holy Spirit. Spend time reading His word and speaking in tongues. Seek God for His word concerning your circumstances and what you desire. Write down what God tells you and make a list of confessions based on His promises to you. These Scriptures are your anchor. Keep your eye on them. They are your sight by which you view your situation. Talk to God regularly, and ask Him what He would like you to know. Ask your request and believe you have received. Take your victory. If doubts come, speak your verses as praises.

Never rely on your feelings and emotions. Only the verses given to you by God. Keep reading the word and meditating on it. That means thinking about it and memorizing it.

Thank you for purchasing *Understanding Faith*. We hope you find it helpful as you live your life by faith. We would love to hear your testimonies! Please consider leaving a review online, if you enjoyed the book. Also, you can check out our website at https://flyingeaglepublications.com for more books and freebies or to share us with your friends.

www.ingramcontent.com/pod-product-compliance
Lightning Source LLC
Chambersburg PA
CBHW071321080526
44587CB00018B/3311